Being sexy is all about attitude, not body type. It's a state of mind.

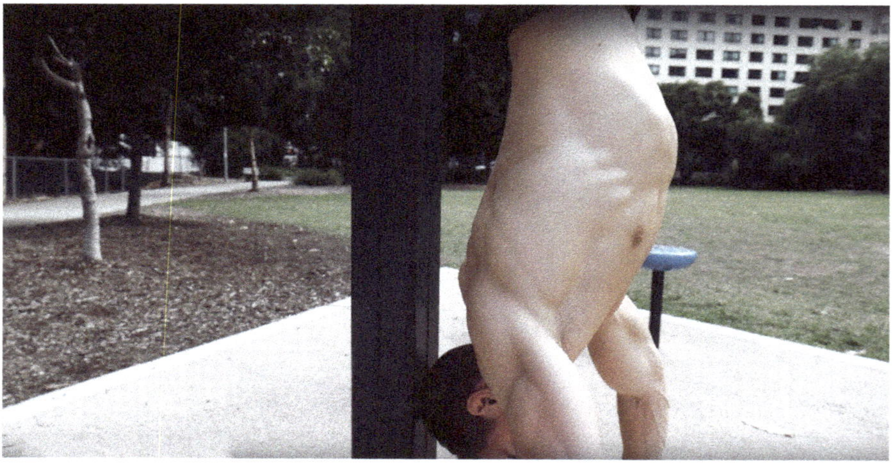

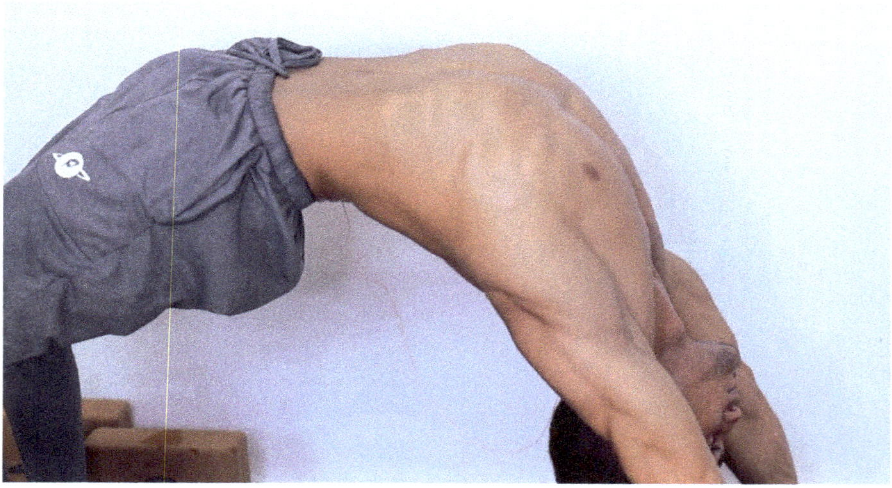

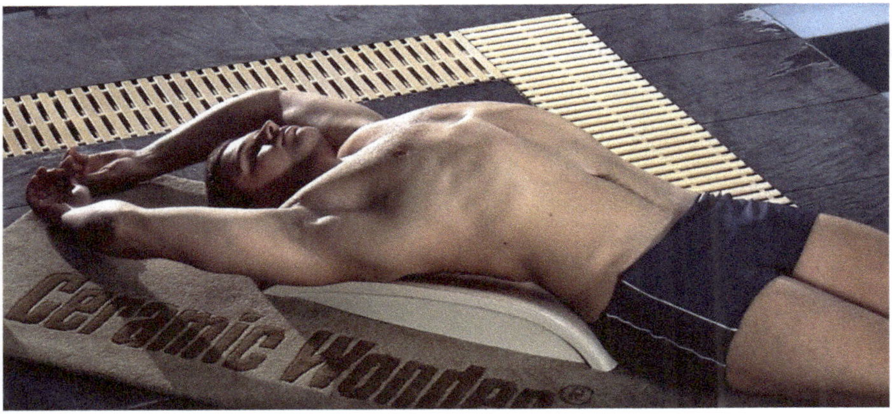
Ceramic Wonder®

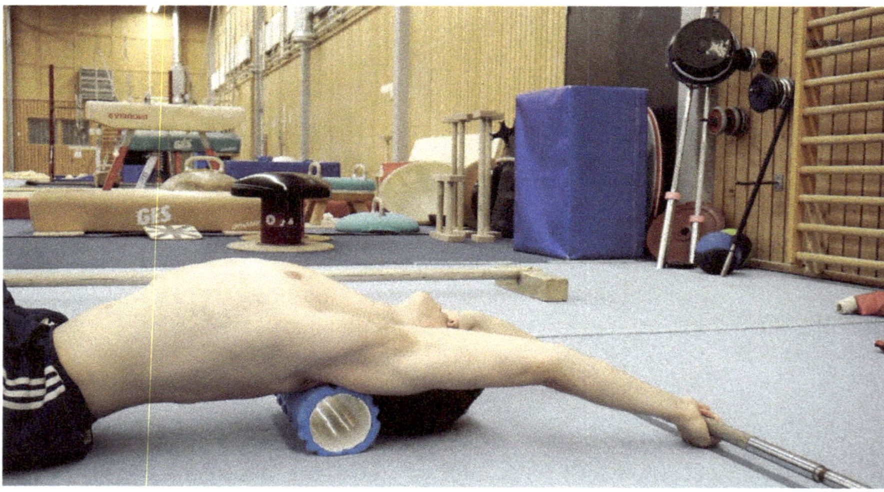

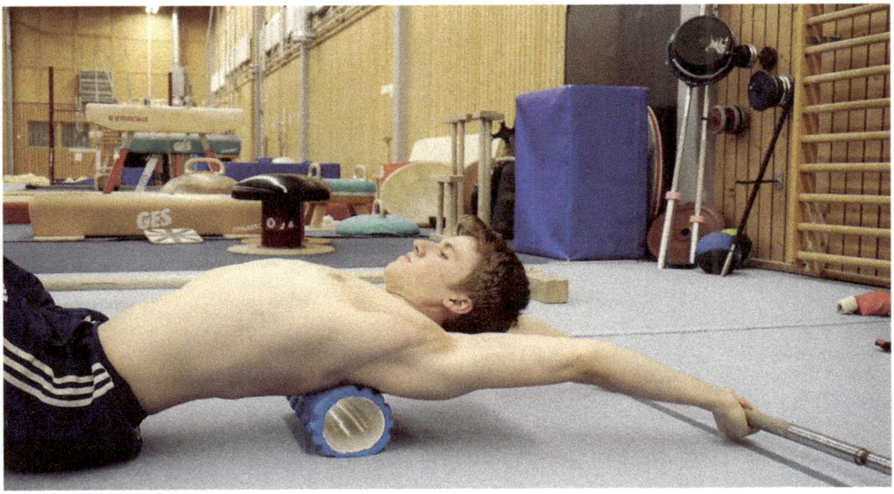
GES

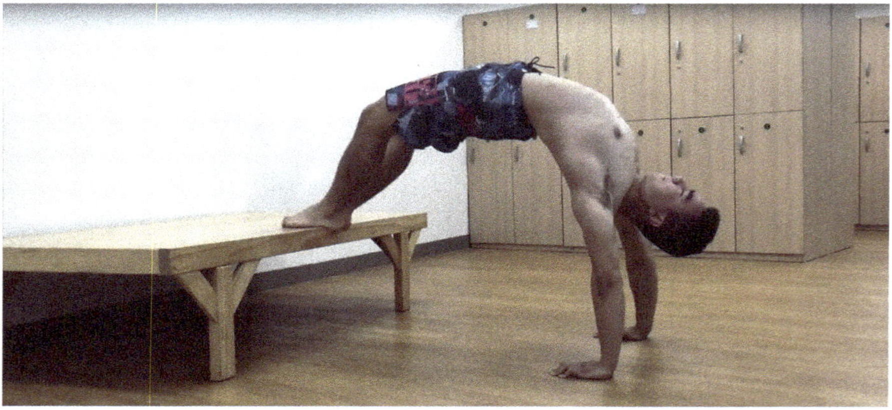

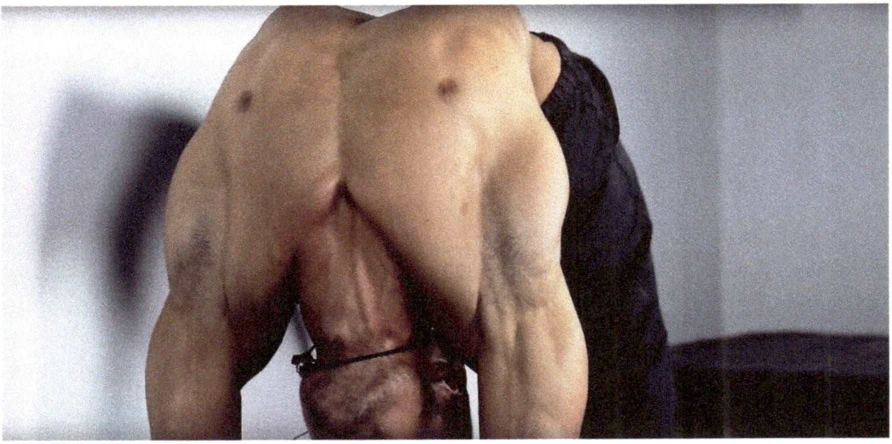

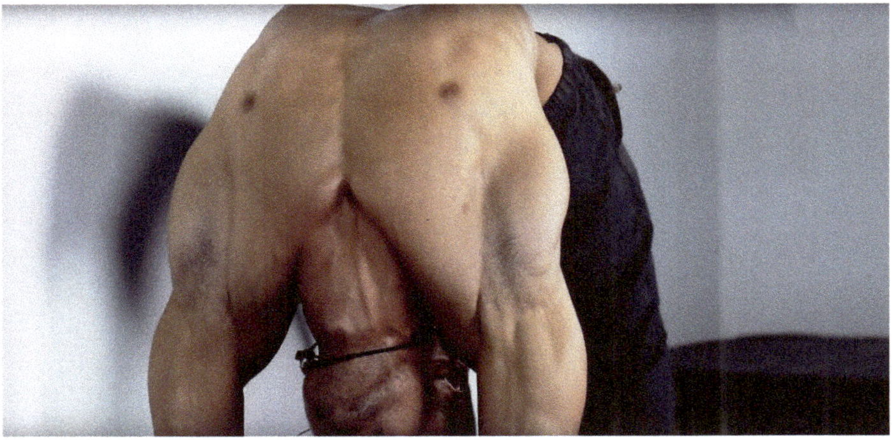

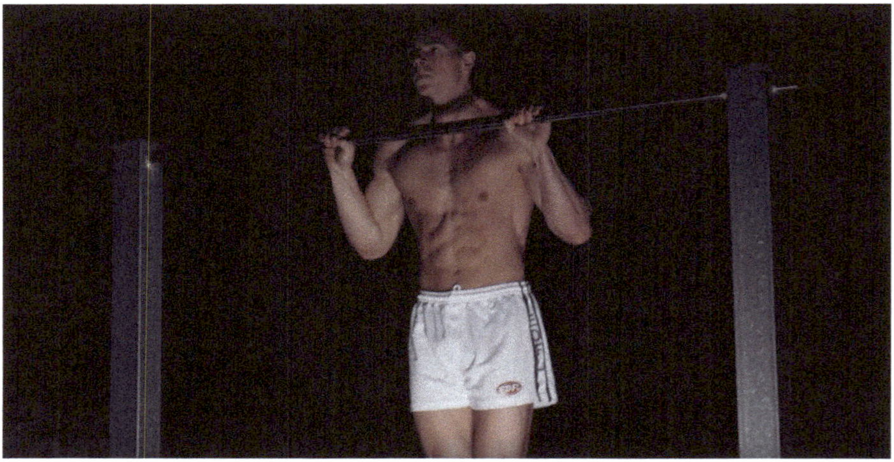

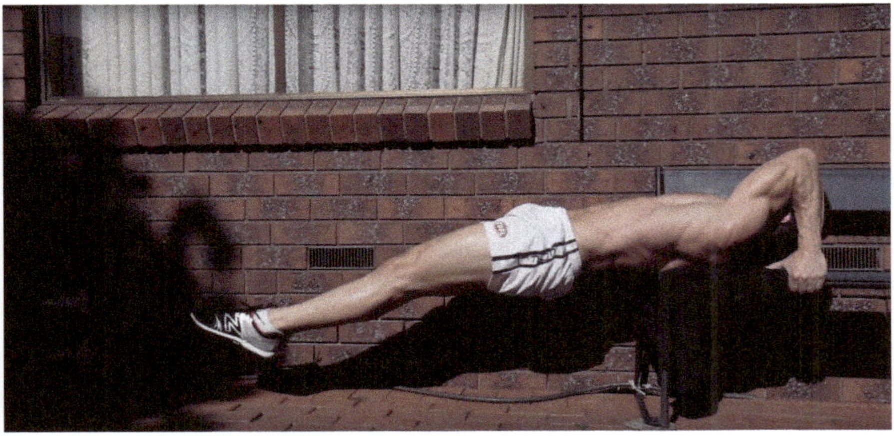

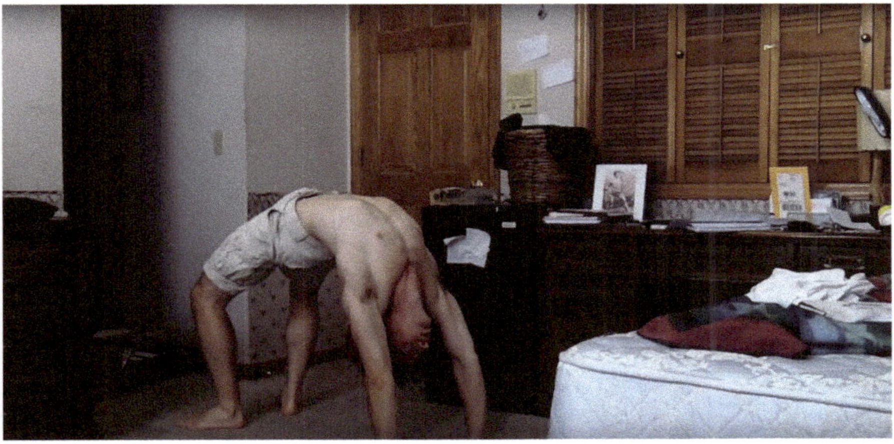

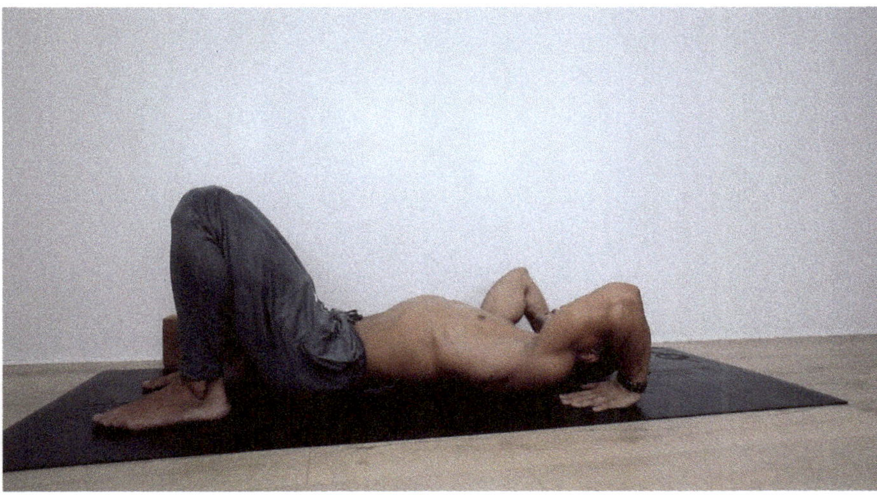

THE MIRAGE

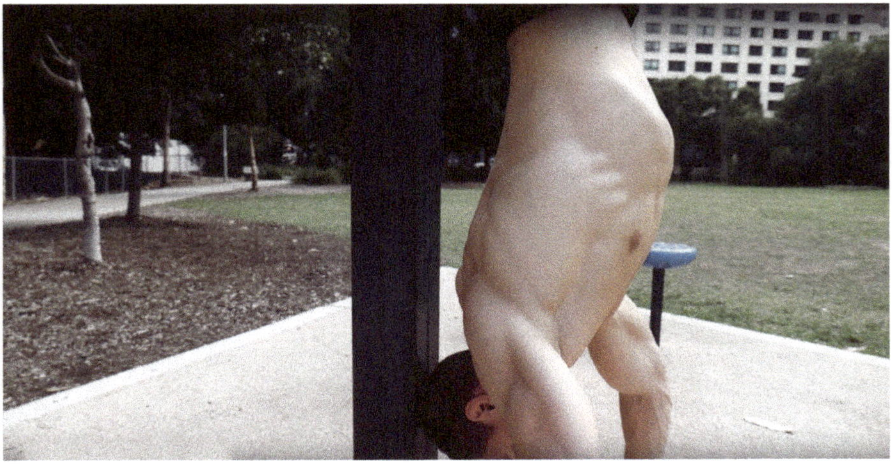

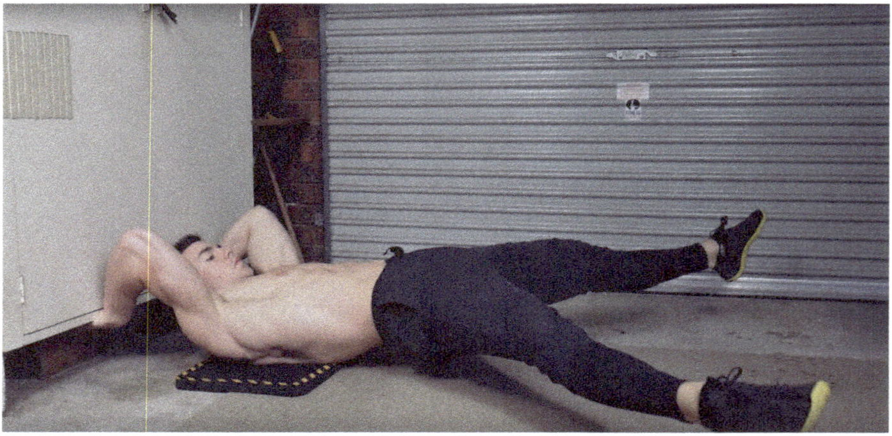

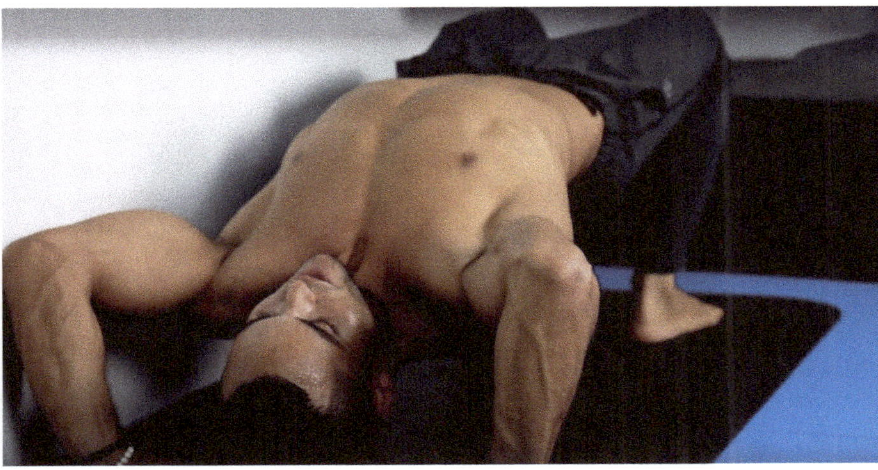

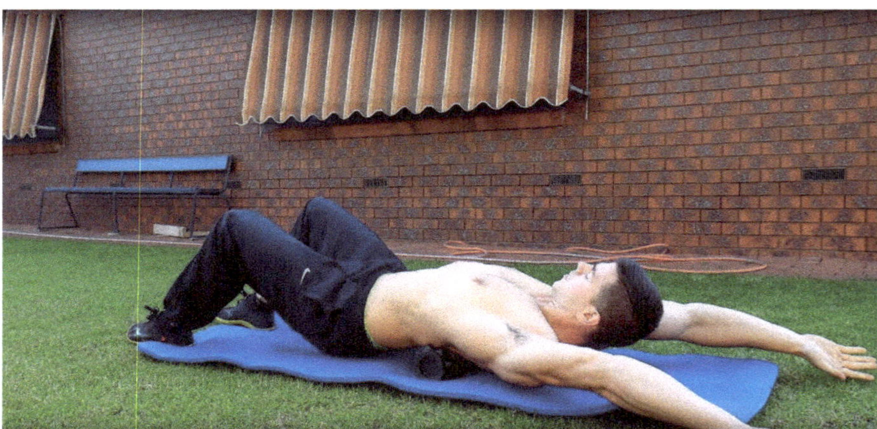

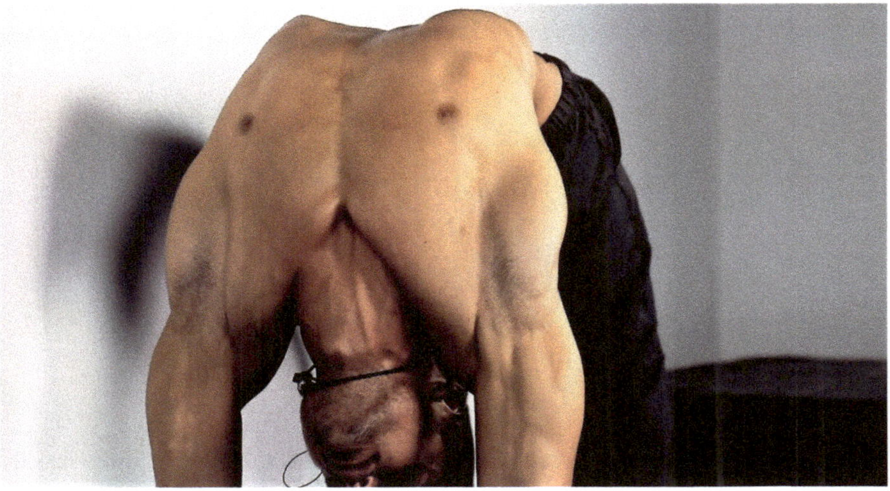

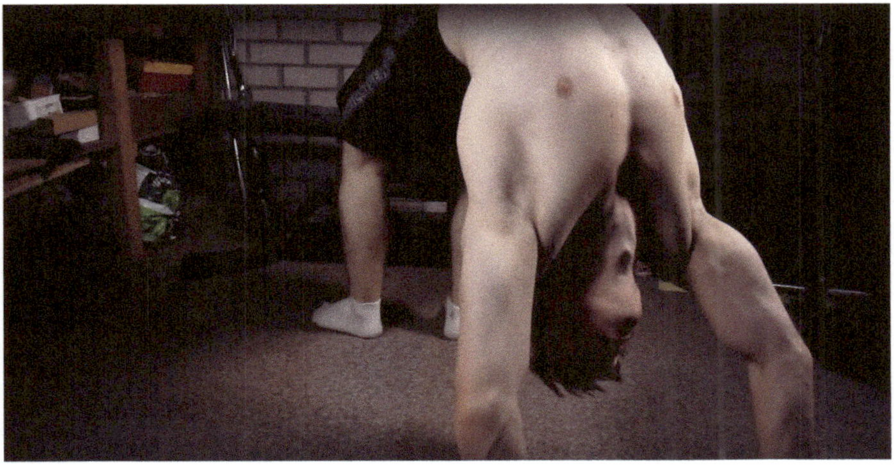

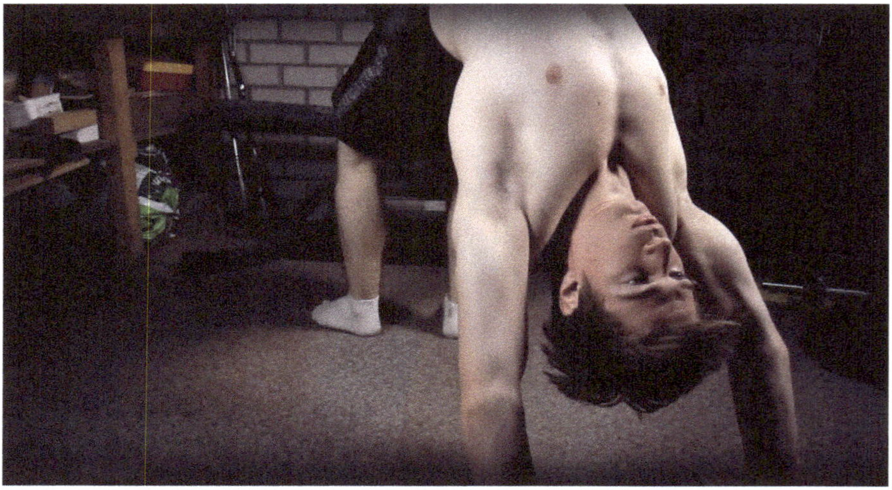

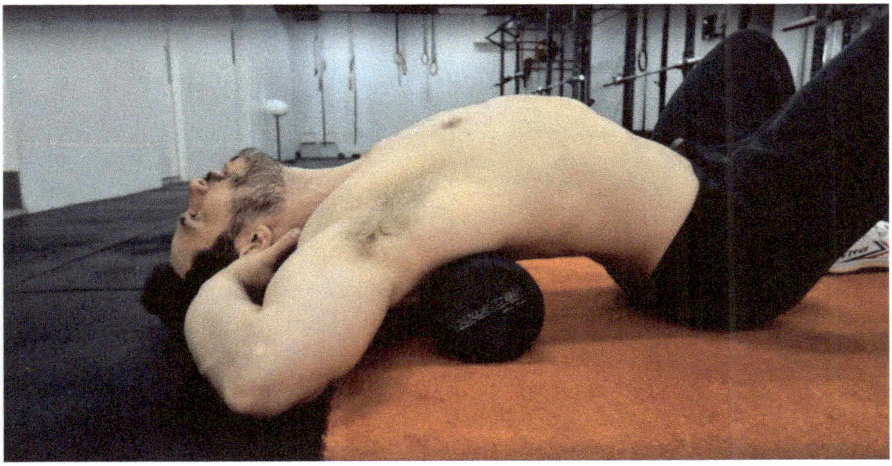

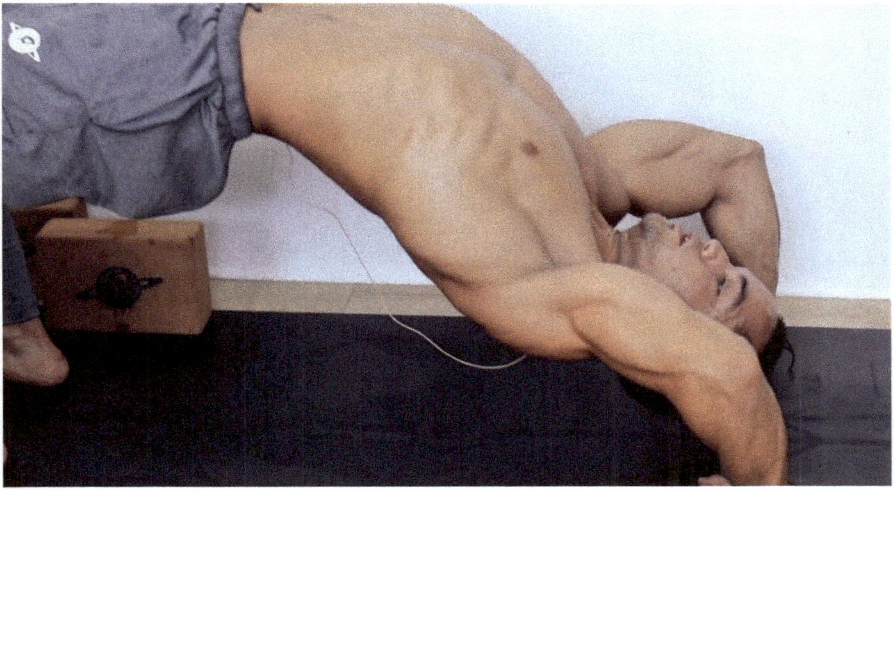

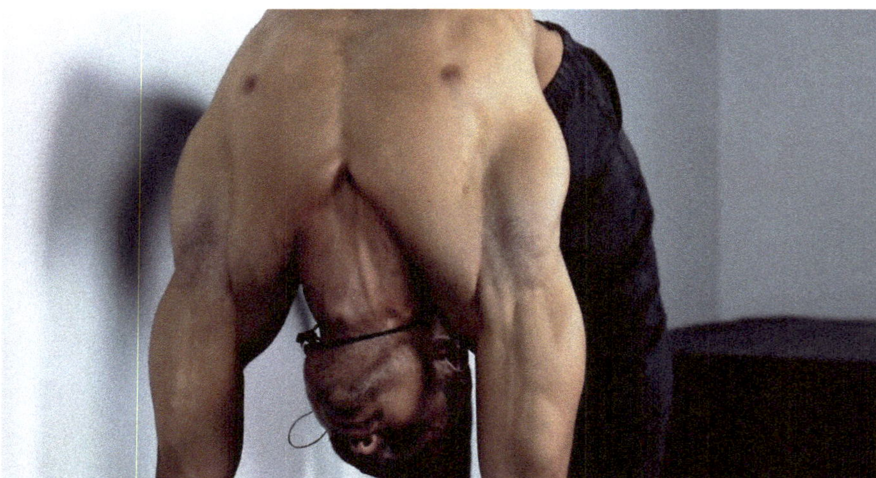

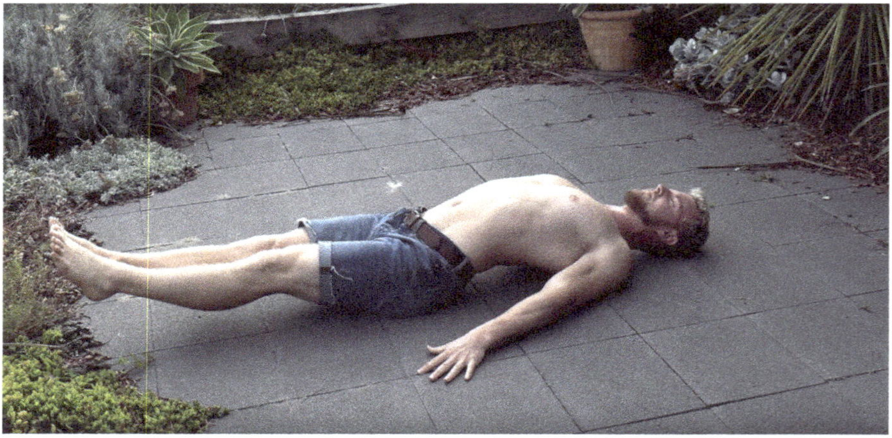

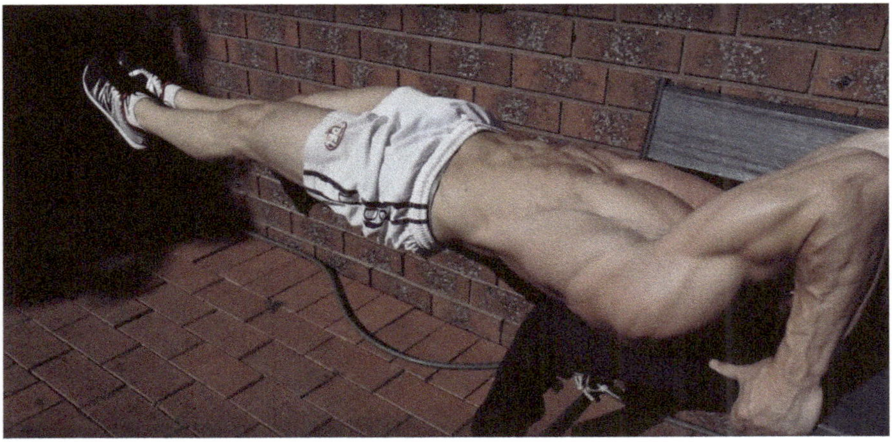

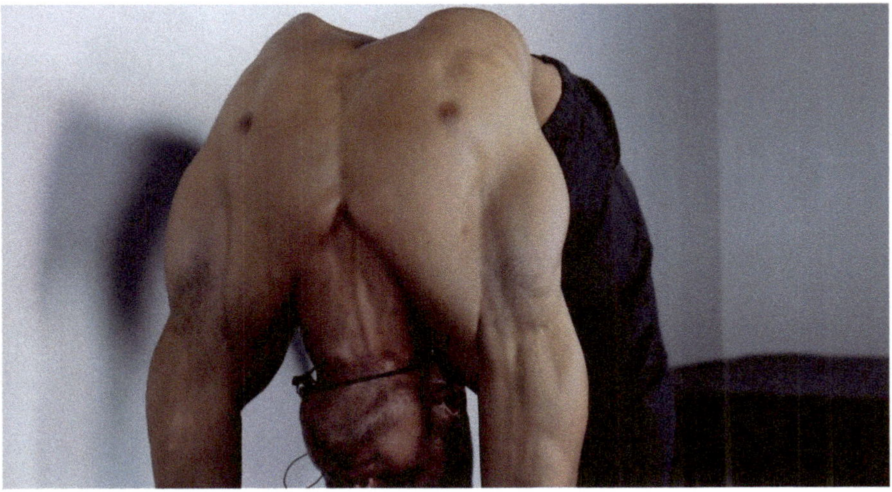

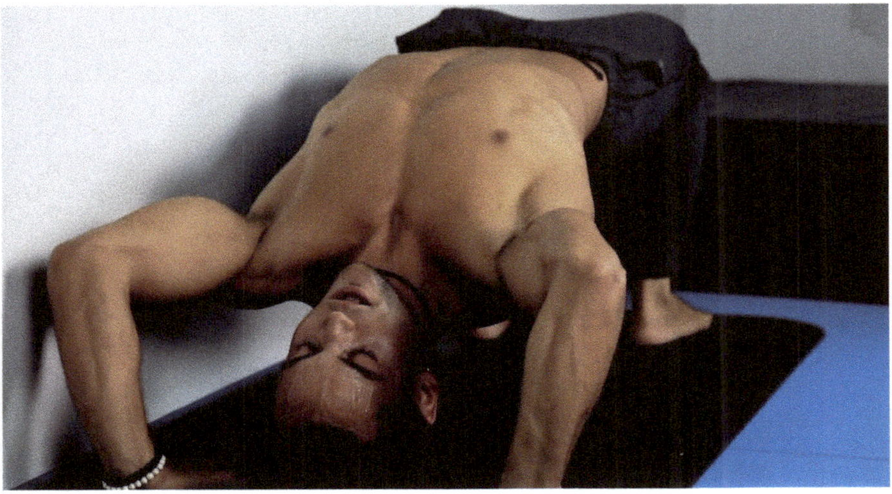

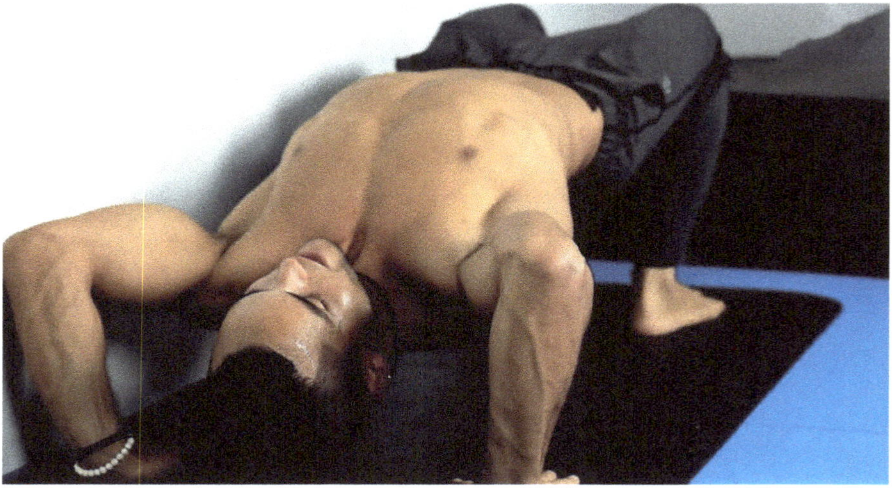

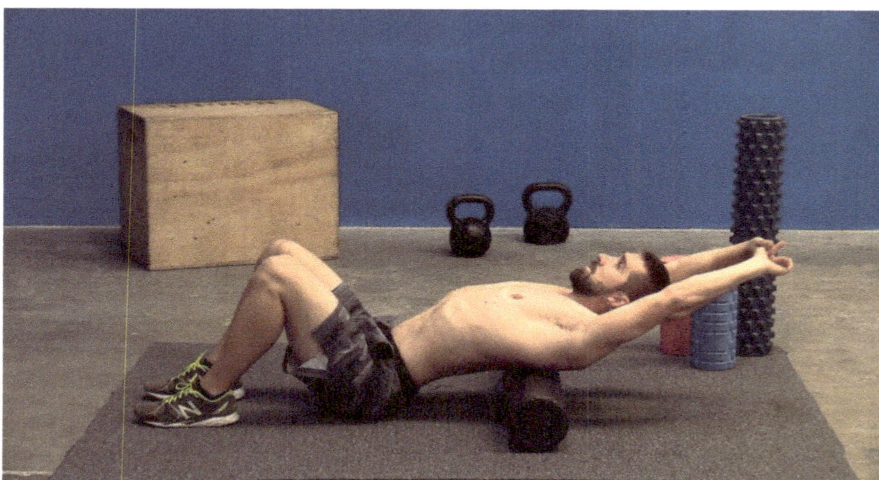

CPSIA information can be obtained
at www.ICGtesting.com
Printed in the USA
BVHW020103140319
542311BV00062B/1471/P

9 780368 395314